MW01482547

MIKE CARPENTER

FLORENCE

*Its History, Its Art,
Its Landmarks*

CONTENTS

HISTORY

Florence is perhaps the "most Italian" city of all. While Milan firmly belongs to continental Europe, Naples is clearly a Mediterranean city, and Rome can be at once a universal hub of imperial history and a provincial town, Florence is the quintessential Italian city. One could argue that everything that gave Italy its unique character was born in Florence or Tuscany. The Italians' language and literature originated here, where this people's artistic genius and spirit of invention also shined to the full. Political ingenuity was not lacking among Florence's citizens, either; one need only think of Niccolò Machiavelli and his *The Prince* – first published in 1532. In a twist of fate, Florence ceased to be the center of Italy's political, artistic, and moral life just when Italy became a nation-state in the middle of the nineteenth century.

From the late Middle Ages to the Renaissance,

Florence grew into a great center of civilization, developing what one could call a peculiar spirit, i.e., an ideal of man and life as a whole that would leave lasting effects on the Italian people and their history. Florentines might even borrow the words spent by the great ancient orator and lawmaker Pericles – who lived in the fifth century BCE – about his fellow Athenians: "We love beauty with simplicity and knowledge without laxity." Over the fourteenth, fifteenth, and sixteenth centuries, Florence could claim to live by that standard, but with a more popular quality completely absent from Athens' ruling aristocracy. In their best moments, the citizens of Florence, though admittedly quarrelsome, were also ingenious, creative, and peaceful, by and large.

Florence never derived its power and wealth from military strength and wars of conquest. Industry and money were the driving forces behind its ascent; merchants and bankers formed its aristocracy. Machiavelli wrote that the city was born in the second century BCE when a group of merchants coming from Fiesole – a small town nestled in the hills northeast of Florence long considered the most affluent center in the whole of Tuscany – settled at the conjunction of the rivers Arno and Mugnone. Archaeological excavation proves the presence of a thriving township in the first century BCE at the time of Roman dictator Lucius Cornelius Sulla, making ancient Florence an established Roman-Etruscan settlement.

Finding itself ideally positioned along the Via Cassia, one of Rome's famed consular roads,

Florence slowly became an important trading hub between Rome, Lucca, Pisa, and Faenza. The Romans called it *Florentia*, and Julius Caesar turned it into a Roman colony. By 287 CE, it was elevated to the capital city of *Tuscia et Umbria* (Etruscan Tuscany and Umbria) and became an episcopal seat in the first half of the fourth century. In 406 CE, the city could repel a siege laid by the Ostrogoths invading Italy from the north under their king, Radagaisus, thanks to the providential intervention of the Roman army led by Stilicho, the most powerful man in the entire Western Roman Empire at the time. A second attempt by the Ostrogoths to take the city happened in 542-543 CE but was equally unsuccessful. On the other hand, King Totila was able to claim an even bigger prize in December 546, when he conquered Rome after a two-year siege.

In later years, Florence became an almost compulsory stop for emperors coming from northern Europe to Rome to be crowned by the pope. It is thought that Charlemagne celebrated Christmas in Florence in 786 during one of his travels to Italy. He was later crowned Emperor of the Romans by Pope Leo III in the ancient St. Peter's Basilica (not the current one) on Christmas Eve of the year 800. During the so-called Carolingian Renaissance of the ninth century, the city gained in importance, becoming the headquarters of the school for the cultural training of the clergy in the Tuscan region in 825 and later the seat of a count directly representing the imperial authority against the powerful marquises of Tuscany.

Florence's ascension to a more prominent role in history began after 1115 when the vastly powerful Marchioness Matilda of Tuscany – also known as Matilda of Canossa – passed away. In the Investiture Controversy, which for fifty years had pitted the emperor against the papacy in a struggle for authority over the empire's bishops, Matilda had been a staunch ally of the pope, and most cities in central Italy – including Florence – had followed her lead. It was Matilda who first granted Florence municipal autonomy, an essential step in the city's rise. A series of victorious struggles of the Florentines against the feudal lords of the countryside allowed the communal magistrates to fortify their rule, and the first consuls were elected starting in 1138. At the time, the power in Florence was in the hands of syndicates of noblemen – the Tower Societies – supported by the clergy and the wealthiest merchant families – the Calimala.

The city's symbol has been universally known as the Lily of Florence for almost one thousand years. In botanical terms, it would be more accurate to call it an iris, the flowering genus to which it belongs. Iris flowers are ubiquitous in the Arno Valley and the hills around Florence, which explains the Florentines' choice. Originally, the coat of arms consisted of a white lily on a red field. In the thirteenth century, after driving the Ghibellines out of town, the winning Guelph party decided to invert the colors in 1266. Today's official coat of arms' appearance was established in 1929 by government decree as follows: "A simple silver oval shield, an open fleur-delis buttoned in red." [see drawing on page 1]

In the twelfth century, Florence inaugurated a policy of territorial expansion at the expense of neighboring cities. The Florentines went on to win short wars against Fiesole (1125), the Guidi counts – who dominated a substantial part of central Italy between Romagna and Tuscany (1143-1153) –, Pisa – a rivalry that would last for over two centuries, until 1406, when Florence definitively subjugated Pisa –, and Empoli, conquered in 1182. After the death of Emperor Henry VI of Swabia in 1197, most political entities in Tuscany formed the Tuscan League, also known as the League of St. Genesius. This was an alliance aimed at earning its members actual sovereignty and independence from imperial rule, not least by pledging to defend each other from the Empire in case of war. In 1198, newly elected Pope Innocent III condemned the League, which represented a danger to his expansionist ambitions in central Italy. However, he had to back down shortly after, eventually placing it under his protection.

From 1215, Florence's political life was dominated by the struggle between the Guelphs and Ghibellines. In the fight over influence between the empire and the papacy, the Guelphs were the "pope's party," whereas the Ghibellines sided with the emperor. Initially, this dispute mainly unfolded in Germany, where both factions contended for the throne. After the election of Frederick I Barbarossa in 1152 had pacified the scene in Germany, the conflict moved south, taking on completely new characteristics. In Tuscany, this struggle showed its true nature of a clash between two competing social classes. While the Ghibelline party represented the feudal reaction against the concept of a free municipality – the form of government that had a pivotal role in the economic and social growth of many of Italy's cities in the late Middle Ages – the Guelphs were instrumental in strengthening the mercantile class, also boosting its weight in the city councils.

In 1248, a forceful imperial intervention in Italy secured a short-lived victory for the Ghibelline party. Upon the death of Emperor Frederick II of Swabia – Frederick Barbarossa's grandson, known to his contemporaries as *stupor mundi* ("astonishment of the world") due to his seemingly endless culture – in 1250, Florence's arts and crafts corporations rebelled against the rule of the aristocrats and established a new form of government called "of the first people," where a "Captain of the People" representing the lower classes would complement the Podestà – a mayor with military command – and the Council of Elders, twelve aldermen coming from the city's aristocracy of commerce who were charged with mediating between the first two in case of disagreements. In this phase of Florence's history, the growth of the city's economic power found a manifest confirmation in the introduction of the gold florin (1252), destined to become medieval Europe's strongest currency for almost three centuries, readily accepted all over the continent.

One advantage Florence enjoyed over its neighboring rivals and competitors was its bourgeois and popular origins, which were in no way linked to the disputes between ecclesiastical and secular feudal lords. Noblemen were only allowed into the city walls after giving up their castles outside of them – which the Florentines considered a threat – and submitting to the laws of the municipality. In the following couple of centuries, Florence made great efforts on the road to a "democratic" ideal, both socially and politically. In 1289, a law was enacted that freed all peasants from serfdom and instituted sharecropping, by which farmers essentially became landowners' partners, thus sharing the fruits of the earth with them. To fully appreciate the magnitude of this breakthrough, one need only consider that peasants in Germany tried to achieve the same rights more than two centuries later by way of revolution, which was put down in a bloodbath. Artisans and merchants, for their part, assembled in guilds and corporations, which were professional and social training centers, too.

The fourteenth century was the golden age of nascent Italian literature. At that time, there was no unitary Italian language. The erudite language, of course, was Latin. Alongside Latin – the language of the few, mainly used in official documents – the inhabitants of the Italian peninsula spoke a host of local dialects we now call medieval vernaculars. That changed in the late Middle Ages – or early Renaissance, depending on which chronology one prefers – thanks to authors like Dante Alighieri, Giovanni Boccaccio, and Francesco Petrarca, all Tuscan by birth and upbringing. Dante's unrivaled narrative poem *Divina Commedia* (*The Divine Comedy*), Boccaccio's *Decameron*, a collection of short stories considered a masterpiece of early Italian prose that achieved widespread influence even outside of Italy's borders, and Petrarca's *Canzoniere*, a voyage in the author's interior life expressed in poetry, helped establish the Tuscan vernacular as the language for all Italians, leaving local dialects to private conversations of the less educated. Dialects, though, never died. To this day, UNESCO estimates that at least thirty dialects are still spoken in the Italian peninsula.

In the arts, Giotto – painter, architect, and sculptor, instrumental in radically renewing the art of painting throughout the Italian peninsula – and the Sienese school launched the great season of Italian painting, which reached its peak in the fifteenth and sixteenth centuries.

But the name that is inextricably linked with the best-known and most glorious period in the history of Florence is that of a family dynasty: the Medici. For about three centuries, from 1434 to 1737, members of the Medici family clan repeatedly ruled the city, from which they were at times banished due to political maneuvering. The origins of this dynasty date back to one Medico, castellan of Potrone in the Mugello area to the northeast of Florence, in the eleventh century. Over the thirteenth and fourteenth centuries, successive generations of Medici started to amass wealth in trade, weaving, and farming, with the first forays into banking on a small scale. The ascension to power and serious wealth started thanks to a banker, Giovanni di Bicci de' Medici, who in 1397 founded the Banco dei Medici (Medici Bank), destined to become the richest and most influential bank on the European continent for the entirety of the fifteenth century.

Thanks to his growing financial clout and as a member of one of Florence's corporations, Giovanni was elected to the *Signoria*, the Council of the Republic of Florence composed of nine members elected among the representatives of the city's professional guilds who wielded all power in town. They assembled in the Palazzo Vecchio (Old Palace), a fortress-like medieval building that was called Palazzo della Signoria at the time. It must be noted that councilmen only served for two months, ensuring a swift replacement ratio that helped reduce opportunities for unwelcome influences from outside as well as corruption. Giovanni was popular among the common people, thanks to his vote to establish a property tax that filled the city coffers at the expense of wealthy landowners like himself.

In the wake of Giovanni's election to the Signoria, the influence of the Medici family began to grow exponentially. Giovanni fathered Cosimo, later called Cosimo il Vecchio (Cosimo the Elder), who eventually became the first real Lord of Florence on behalf of his family. After his father died in 1429, Cosimo found himself at the head of the Medici House. Having realized that his family was too wealthy and prominent to operate without political protection, he set about to increase his influence in the city's government, always remaining in the shadows as the puppeteer of trusted figures holding key institutional positions on his behalf. By leveraging his wealth, his reputation as a generous patron of the arts, and several marriages of convenience, he was able to form a strong alliance against the faction of the oligarchs then dominating the city's political life, led by the Albizzi, Strozzi, Peruzzi, and Castellani families.

In September 1433, Cosimo's plotting behind the scenes resulted in him being sentenced to exile after risking capital punishment based on spurious charges. He first settled in Padua, then Venice, where the Medici Bank had one of its most vital branches. Although he was supposed to stay away from Florence for ten years, his exile was short-lived. Only one year later, in September 1434, a new Signoria, much more well-disposed toward the Medici, took office. At the time, its members were drawn by lot, and Cosimo's rivals lacked the resources to effectively influence proceedings in one way or the other. On 6 October 1434, Cosimo returned to Florence in triumph, acclaimed by the people of Florence, who much preferred the tolerant Medici to the snobbish and strict Albizzi and their allies.

Once back in town, Cosimo quickly became the dominant figure in Florence's political life for thirty years. He had his enemies banished or excluded from public office while his loyalists rose to the highest positions in the state. In 1458, he created the Council of the Hundred to safeguard his power best. The reign of Cosimo de' Medici is often referred to as a "crypto-lordship" since he never held official positions of power in the city. He always operated behind the scenes; still, there was no doubt about where the real power lay. During his time as the *de facto* head of Florentine politics, the Republic, initially allied with Venice against the expansionist policy of Duke Filippo Maria Visconti of Milan, turned to an alliance with his successor Francesco Sforza – who had a friendly relationship with Cosimo – and France.

Cosimo loved the arts and did not hesitate to invest much of his enormous private wealth to beautify his hometown and make it glorious, calling artists to work in the city and building public and religious buildings. He was active in many fields, promoting agriculture with competence, increasing trade, and commissioning critical public works, among them the ones to improve the navigability of the Arno River. Under his rule, the Medici banking house became one of Europe's richest and most influential, and Florence was one of the continent's most thriving cities. He was a protector of writers and artists; he built churches, chapels, palaces, and splendid villas; he opened and gave impetus to public libraries.

After Cosimo died in 1464, the Signoria proclaimed him *Pater Patriae*, a Latin expression meaning Father of the Homeland. His funerary monument can be seen inside the crypt of the Basilica of San Lorenzo, one of the city's oldest churches. By all accounts, his administration of the Republic laid the foundations for the city's golden age that reached its peak under the government of his nephew, Lorenzo the Magnificent.

Cosimo's son and heir was Piero, who only reigned – informally, just like his father – for five years before dying prematurely in 1469. His nickname was Piero il Gottoso, which means Piero the Gouty, since he suffered from gout, a complex form of arthritis quite common at the time that is characterized by sudden, severe attacks of pain, swelling, redness, and tenderness in one or more joints, most often in the big toe. Piero proved to be a wise ruler, capable of forcefully suppressing a coup attempt masterminded by the outrageously wealthy merchant Luca Pitti (see Palazzo Pitti below, the family palace in Florence) and governing the city effectively. Still, it was his son Lorenzo de' Medici, later dubbed Lorenzo il Magnifico, who earned the House of Medici the consecration to everlasting glory.

Lorenzo is, without a doubt, the best-known and most admired member of his dynasty. He was not only a skilled politician who ruled the city for twenty-three years as the *de facto* ruler of Florence, but also a humanist and philosopher, lover and patron of the arts, and even an artist himself. In a nutshell, he embodied almost every virtue of a Renaissance man. As the uncrowned prince of a proud and thriving community, he earned his family and city a central role in a turbulent time for Italy's politics, when alliances changed overnight and conspiracies and betrayals were a frequent occurrence.

Lorenzo was born on New Year's Day 1449, at a time when his grandfather, Cosimo the Elder, had secured the support of several local politicians and the all-important trade and craft guilds by setting himself up as a staunch ally of the ordinary people and the bourgeoisie in the face of perceived slights at the hands of the aristocratic class. Florence had always been a republic, but in practice, it was ruled by an oligarchy of wealthy families adept at forging the right alliances – both in town and with other powerful cities – to accumulate ever-growing influence. Cosimo had much strengthened the Medici Bank founded by his father, thanks to a successful expansion strategy that had resulted in the creation of several branches throughout Europe and his ties to the papacy, of which he was the primary lender.

Both his grandfather Cosimo and his ailing father Piero deemed Lorenzo the family's best bet for a bright future. They entrusted him with important roles in their banking business from a young age. At the early age of sixteen, Lorenzo traveled to Milan, Venice, Rome, and Naples on official business, partly to deal with financial matters and partly to meet sovereigns and rulers with whom Florence was allied or hoped to be. When his father died, a twenty-year-old Lorenzo was ready to take the reins of Florence's most prominent family.

Lorenzo inherited wealth and power from his father (and grandfather), but his mother – Lucrezia Tornabuoni – was equally important in shaping his life and, thus, Florence's future. As a highly respected and educated woman who wrote poetry and loved being surrounded by artists and intellectuals such as painter Sandro Botticelli – author of *The*

Birth of Venus –, poet Poliziano, and philosopher Pico della Mirandola – a leading figure of Italian humanism – Lucrezia taught her son a taste for beautiful, refined things. Furthermore, she was always an ally Lorenzo could count on and even chose his wife, Clarice Orsini, whom Lorenzo wedded in a marriage of convenience. There had already been two popes in the Orsini family, and a third – Pope Benedict XIII – would follow in 1724. Even Lorenzo and Clarice's second male child, Giovanni, was destined to wear the white robe as Pope Leo X.

The most severe challenge to the reign of the Medici came in 1478 when Lorenzo was only twenty-nine. In those years, the ultra-rich Pazzi family was the only family with the means and the will to dispute Lorenzo's primacy over Florence. The enmity between the two families climaxed after Pope Sixtus IV Della Rovere's election to the papal throne in 1471. In 1473, the Duke of Milan, Galeazzo Maria Sforza, put up the city of Imola for sale, roughly fifty miles northeast of Florence and near Bologna. The pope was interested in buying it to expand his possessions in central Italy but lacked the necessary funds. Hence, he asked the Medici Bank to bankroll him. Lorenzo refused since he was wary of being surrounded by papal territories and wanted to keep open the all-important trading routes to the north, where Florence had entered into lucrative commercial agreements with Milan and Venice. An enraged Sixtus IV turned to the Pazzi family for financial support.

The Pazzi Bank became the pope's go-to

financial institution, replacing the Medici Bank, but hostilities between the two leading Florentine dynasties were far from over. In 1477, Lorenzo found a way to take revenge upon his rivals for helping the pope to add Imola to his dominions a few years earlier. When Giovanni de' Pazzi's wealthy father-in-law died, Lorenzo passed legislation preventing daughters from inheriting – absent male heirs – in favor of male cousins. By making this law retroactive, he ensured that Giovanni's wife, Beatrice Borromei, could not inherit her father's massive fortune, adding it to the Pazzi estate. That was probably the tipping point in the whole saga.

Interestingly, it wasn't the wronged Giovanni who hatched the conspiracy to assassinate Lorenzo and his brother Giuliano, but two different members of the Pazzi family clan: Jacopo de' Pazzi – one of Florence's wealthiest citizens – and his nephew Francesco, Sixtus IV's personal banker. They planned to poison both brothers on 25 April 1478 during a banquet at Villa Medici in Fiesole, Lorenzo's country mansion just outside Florence. The two dynasties were related through marriage (celebrated in 1468, before relations soured), so some members of the Pazzi family were always invited to such events. Fortunately for Lorenzo, the conspiracy was destined to go sideways very quickly.

The plan was ruined by an accident that happened to Giuliano, who suffered an injury during a hunting trip the day before the banquet, following which he preferred to stay in bed to recover. The conspirators were forced to hastily devise an emergency plan. They decided they would kill the Medici brothers the next day, which was a Sunday, in the city's cathedral – Santa Maria del Fiore – where all prominent citizens of Florence gathered every week for Sunday mass. To reach their goal, they did not hesitate to involve two priests, which turned out to be a bad idea. Francesco de' Pazzi was charged with killing Giuliano de' Medici with the help of a friend of his, the merchant Bernardo Bandini Baroncelli. At the same time, the two treacherous priests were supposed to act as hitmen and take care of Lorenzo during mass.

On the fateful day, Giuliano did not attend church, forcing Francesco and Bernardo to fetch him at the Medici Palace to take him to the cathedral. At the elevation, when everybody was kneeling, the two priests involved in the plot attacked Lorenzo but were not able to cause any significant damage due to their inexperience in handling knives. Aided by his entourage, Lorenzo could escape into the sacristy with his wife and mother. Giuliano was less lucky. Francesco and Bernardo jumped on him and stabbed him repeatedly, leaving him dead in a pool of blood.

Meanwhile, Jacopo de' Pazzi had marched on Palazzo della Signoria – the seat of government – with a group of mercenaries. In the square in front, he proclaimed "freedom from the Medici tyranny." But the people's reaction was not at all what he expected. Shouting "palle, palle" – which means "balls, balls," a reference to the Medici coat of arms, containing six bezants in the shape of balls – the citizens of Florence gave chase to the conspirators. Jacopo de' Pazzi was among the few to escape with his life, reaching the papal troops encamped not far from the city to take over in case of a successful coup.

A wounded Francesco de' Pazzi – who was captured at his home soon after Giuliano's assassination – and Francesco Salviati – the Archbishop of Pisa who hated Lorenzo for denying him the more prestigious post in Tuscany's capital and had participated in the plot – were soon hanging from a window at Palazzo della Signoria. In the following days, the town magistrates proceeded ruthlessly against the traitors. Many were apprehended, tortured, and hanged. Bernardo Bandini could initially escape to Constantinople but was handed over to Florence by the Ottomans in December 1479. He was hanged, of course, his dangling body immortalized in a drawing by a young Leonardo da Vinci absorbed in his anatomy studies (now kept in the Musée Bonnat-Helleu in Bayonne, France).

Following the wide-ranging revenge ordered by Lorenzo, which cost many lives, and furious about a major blow to his ambitions, Pope Sixtus IV excommunicated several members of the Medici family and demanded the release of the prisoners who had participated in the plot and the handing over of those responsible for the violence that had followed the failed coup. Predictably, Lorenzo refused, which caused a two-year war between Florence and the Papal States with its various allies. The Ottoman invasion of Puglia (Apulia) in southern Italy in July 1480 concentrated everyone's attention on a different, common enemy. The Medici recovered all possessions previously lost during the war in exchange for financial compensation and military support against the invading Turks.

However, Lorenzo de' Medici did not earn his moniker of "il Magnifico" – "the Magnificent" – on the battlefield. Instead, it was his love for the arts and his role as a patron of some of the greatest painters, sculptors, and architects that ever lived to secure his place in history. From a young age, Lorenzo had always been surrounded by intellectuals and artists in his mother's circle, and he grew up well-versed in rhetoric, poetry, and music. Poetry, in particular, was his great passion, resulting in several romantic sonnets and bucolic lyrics that reveal Lorenzo's belief in the fragility of life and the need to enjoy it.

His most famous verses are from his *Song for Bacchus* and read:

> *How beautiful our youth is,*
> *That's always flying by us!*
> *Who'd be happy, let him be:*
> *Nothing's sure about tomorrow.*

Under his protection, the Renaissance's absolute champions could develop their talents and thrive, giving the world an endless parade of unmatched masterpieces. Suffice it to mention three names of worldwide and undying importance: Leonardo da

Vinci, Sandro Botticelli, and Michelangelo Buonarroti. Perhaps his most significant endeavor was the Academy of Art he founded in the Garden of San Marco (now gone and remembered by a plaque), possibly the first of its kind in Europe. Here, Lorenzo met a very young Michelangelo, immediately realizing the immense talent of the Renaissance genius.

Lorenzo's patronage of the arts also had an important political function. Besides his desire to make Florence the brightest light in Italy's late Middle Ages, he knew that his ambitious public projects would not only find favor with the citizenry but also secure the gratitude and support of the arts, crafts, and trade guilds, whose representatives actively participated in municipal politics and constituted Lorenzo's main power base. Prominent intellectuals like the poet and philologist Poliziano, Marsilio Ficino – a philosopher and astrologist –, and Pico della Mirandola – one of Renaissance's best-known philosophers and humanists – all belonged to the circle around Florence's undisputed leader.

Politically, Lorenzo had emerged strengthened from the clash with the papacy. After Sixtus IV died in 1484, and thanks to his alliance with the Kingdom of Naples, Lorenzo became an essential mediator between great powers on the Italian peninsula. In his personal life, though, he took two heavy hits. His mother, Lucrezia Tornabuoni, died in 1482, followed six years later by his wife, Clarice. Meanwhile, Lorenzo had begun showing symptoms of gout, the same disease that had killed his father. A loss of reputation and authority marred his later years. The war against Pope Sixtus IV had cost a fortune, leaving a big hole in the state finances. Furthermore, the Dominican friar Girolamo Savonarola was wreaking havoc in Florence with his fierce criticism of the way of life of the privileged few and the clergy, also taking aim at Lorenzo himself for what he considered an ostentatious and decadent lifestyle inspired by classicizing paganism.

Lorenzo de' Medici, forever remembered as the Magnificent, died on April 8, 1492, aged only forty-three, six months before Cristopher Columbus reached the Americas. One month earlier, his second-born Giovanni had been appointed cardinal. One day, he would become pope with the name of Leo X. With Lorenzo's passing, the Medici lost much of their clout in the city's politics, and Florence was pushed to the margins of events in Italy. From 1494 to 1559, the Italian peninsula became the privileged battlefield where French and Spanish sovereigns competed for supremacy over Europe.

From time to time, a member of the Medici family still ruled the Grand Duchy of Tuscany. Cosimo I de' Medici, who was Duke of Florence from 1537 to 1569 and later Grand Duke of Tuscany until 1574, during his time in power annexed the Republic of Siena, reorganized the public administration, reclaimed lands, and improved the ports of Livorno and Portoferraio. Ferdinand I, who ruled from 1587 to 1609, was instrumental in raising the profile of the University of Pisa, which was made illustrious in those days by a man widely considered the founder of modern science – the physicist, mathematician, and astronomer Galileo Galilei.

In 1738, after the last of the Medici grand dukes – Gian Gastone – had died, Tuscany passed to the Habsburg-Lorraine royal family. The King of France had assigned the grand duchy to Francis Stephen of Lorena in exchange for the Lorraine region in France, which he had annexed to his kingdom. Under the new rule, Florence developed through a series of reforms and never lost its luster. Traversing Italy for his famous Grand Tour, Johann Wolfgang Goethe – Germany's greatest poet – thus wrote about Florence:

On the morning of the 23rd, at ten o'clock according to our time, emerging from the Apennines, we saw at our feet the broad valley in which Florence lies, incredibly fertile and dotted with villas and houses as far as the eye can see. I hurriedly crossed the city, saw the Cathedral, the Baptistery. The world that opens up to me here is entirely new and unknown, and I don't want to linger in it. The location of the Boboli Gardens is delightful. I left just as quickly as I entered. The city bears witness to the wealth of the people who built it; one realizes it has enjoyed a happy series of governments. Generally, one is struck by the beautiful and grandiose appearance that public works have in Tuscany, the roads, the bridges. Everything is solid and clean at the same time; an attempt is made to combine practicality, utility, and elegance; everywhere, one notices a lively diligence.

In modern times, Florence briefly was the capital city of the newly formed Kingdom of Italy from February 1865 to February 1871, when Rome replaced her after the annexation of the Papal States. Its history as the cradle of the Italian language and its geographical position right in the peninsula's center made it an ideal candidate at the time.

In the early hours of 4 November 1966, disaster struck this incomparable city, one of the most beautiful in the world. Several days of heavy rainfall throughout Tuscany and much of Italy meant that the soil could no longer absorb the incredible volume of water, and rivers threatened to overflow. On a Friday morning before dawn, the Arno, the river flowing westbound to the south of the city center, spilled over, flooding much of Florence with a mind-boggling volume of water and mud. The Arno's entire water catchment area was involved, both upstream and downstream of the city. At 2:30 in the night, it was clear that something serious was about to happen. By 7:00 am, the typography of *La Nazione*, Florence's leading newspaper, stood under fifteen feet of water. At 9:00 am, the river's muddy waters reached Piazza del Duomo, the very heart of the Tuscan capital. At its height, the flooding swept up everything, traveling at a speed of up to forty miles per hour. Footage from the era is as terrifying as it is heartbreaking.

On 6 November 1966, the inhabitants of Florence could breathe again. Once the waters receded, they left behind an astonishing 600,000 tons of mud, covering every corner of this storied city.

Thirty-five people lost their lives, seventeen of which were in Florence proper and another eighteen in the province. In the Santa Croce district, via dei Neri, a plaque commemorates the highest point reached by the flood: 4 meters and 92 centimeters (sixteen feet).

PIAZZA DEL DUOMO

Right in the middle of town, piazza del Duomo (Cathedral Square) is home to three of Florence's most famous landmarks, each deserving of a detailed introduction: the Cathedral itself [see cover image], the Baptistery of Saint John, and Giotto's Campanile. Unfortunately, visitors cannot enjoy a generous perspective toward those undisputed marvels of architecture, such as the vast squares leading to St. Peter's Basilica in Rome, the Duomo in Milan, or St. Mark's Basilica in Venice. The area comprising the cathedral is crowded with houses since there has never been a massive urban intervention such as the one around St. Peter's that freed the façade of the largest church in the world from an entire medieval neighborhood obstructing its view. In fact, only minor demolition work to make place for the new cathedral was undertaken.

In ancient and early medieval times, what is now Cathedral Square was on Florence's outskirts; with the city's growth from the eleventh century on, it slowly became a nodal point in the urban fabric. At the end of the thirteenth century, when the ancient Cathedral of Santa Reparata from the fifth century gave way to the new one called Santa Maria del Fiore (Saint Mary of the Flower), the square gained the role of the space where the most important events in the life of the city took place. The spiritual heart of Florence and a UNESCO World Heritage Site, the square is nothing less than an open-air museum, assembling a head-spinning concentration of history, art, and unmitigated beauty in a few hundred feet.

Up to the present day, the square has maintained its role as the stage of significant public events of the Florentine tradition, such as the spectacular Cavalcata dei Magi every year on 6 January – a colorful procession opened by the Three Wise Men on horseback followed by up to seven hundred extras, starting at piazza Pitti and ending at the Duomo – and the elaborate Scoppio del Carro, on the morning of Easter Sunday, a tradition going back almost one thousand years meant to commemorate the heroic feat of Pazzino de' Pazzi (from the Pazzi family met in the previous chapter), who was said to have been the first crusader to climb over the walls of Jerusalem during the First Crusade, in 1099.

DUOMO OF FLORENCE
GIOTTO'S CAMPANILE

The Cathedral of Santa Maria del Fiore (a minor basilica), which almost everybody simply calls Duomo – a word derived from the Latin *domus*, meaning house, hence "the house of the Lord" – is a jewel of late-Gothic and early-Renaissance architecture. At the time of its completion, in the mid-fifteenth century, it was the largest Catholic church in the world (St. Peter's in Rome dates to 1626). It can accommodate up to 30,000 people inside. To this day, its incredible, awe-inspiring cupola by Filippo Brunelleschi is the largest masonry dome ever constructed.

Among the three or four largest churches in the world, the basilica has a three-nave plan leading into a large presbytery surmounted by the immense octagonal dome by Brunelleschi. Three apses surround the presbytery, each composed of five radial chapels. The cathedral measures 544 feet (166 meters) in outer length and 141 feet (43 meters) in width, which becomes 311 feet (95 meters) at the transept. The internal height is 147 feet (45 meters) and doubles under the dome. Including the cross at its very top, the famous cupola is 382 feet (116 meters) tall. It is possible to go up the dome from the inside, climbing 463 steps, to admire up close the stunning frescos – the largest frescoed surface in the world – by Giorgio Vasari, one of Renaissance's greatest masters. The dedication to Saint Mary of the Flower clearly alludes to Florence's symbol, the iris.

The Duomo stands on the foundations of the prior cathedral, the much smaller Santa Reparata, which was dedicated to Reparata, a girl of noble descent who was tortured to death in Palestine during Emperor Decius's persecution against the Christians in the years 250 to 251 CE. The remains of the ancient church – which were brought to light during a major excavation campaign conducted between 1965 and 1973 – can be visited after descending a staircase on the right of the central nave after the first pillar. The first stone of the new cathedral was laid on 8 September 1296, on the feast of the Nativity of the Virgin Mary. After contemplating a reinforcement and enlargement of the old church, Florence's Signoria (the city government) opted for a comprehensive reconstruction instead. The desire to eclipse the cathedrals of rival cities – such as

Siena and Pisa – certainly played a role in the decision.

The first project was by architect, sculptor, and urbanist Arnolfo di Cambio, mainly active in Rome and Florence. Arnolfo had already built the city's new walls and had been involved in numerous renovation programs of civil and religious buildings in town. His main contribution to the new cathedral was its façade (not the current one), which was erected while Santa Reparata still served as the city's cathedral. In fact, the old name was used at least until 1412, when the Signoria imposed the new denomination by decree. It is believed that the church designed by Arnolfo was quite a bit smaller than the one subsequently built, which is the result of a later project.

After Arnolfo died in 1302, work on the new cathedral stopped for over thirty years. Only the discovery in 1330 of the relics of Saint Zenobius – venerated as the first bishop of Florence in the early fifth century CE – under the old cathedral gave fresh impetus to construction. In 1334, architect and painter Giotto di Bondone – universally known as Giotto – was entrusted with completing the church. Giotto had already created the marvelous frescos decorating the Basilica of Saint Francis in Assisi and the cycle of frescos which make the Chapel of the Scrovegni in Padua one of the absolute masterpieces in the history of painting. He was the most important living artist at the time. In Florence, he started by focusing on the bell tower, the world-famous Campanile.

* * *

Giotto's Campanile is the cathedral's bell tower and stands to the right of its façade, 278 feet (85 meters) tall with a square base 49 feet (15 meters) wide. Its foundations had already been dug in 1298, but Giotto provided the tower's design and supervised the initial construction phase, starting in 1334. He died only three years later, in January 1337, leaving his pupil Andrea Pisano in charge of completing the project. In the end, the Campanile was only wrapped up in 1359 by Francesco Talenti, the architect appointed in 1351 as foreman of the entire worksite after Pisano died in 1348.

The Campanile is a masterpiece of Italian Gothic. Its exterior façades are entirely covered in white, red, and green marble, adorned with stylized flower drawings and geometric motifs. Giotto's hand is only visible in the bell tower's first two levels, where each of the four sides is decorated with a long series of bas-reliefs representing traditional scenes, hexagonal on the base and diamond-shaped on the level above. Most were realized by Andrea Pisano, but the beautiful iconographic scheme was Giotto's idea.

The bas-reliefs are arranged by theme on the Campanile's four sides. On the northern side, the one toward the cathedral's entrance, evocative characters of the past are depicted, representing as many arts – such as Plato and Aristotle for philosophy, the Athenian Phidias for sculpture, Pythagoras for astrology, and so on. One level up, the seven sacraments are shown: baptism, atonement, marriage, confirmation, Eucharist, anointing of the sick, and sacred order. On the western side, facing the Baptistery of St. John, there is a series of seven mythological scenes, such as the creation of Adam and Eve, and Noah and the invention of wine. The solar system's seven planets known at the time – including the moon – grace the tablets on the second level.

Facing south, seven other arts were crafted by Andrea Pisano, such as astronomy, medicine, horse riding, etc. The three theological virtues – faith, hope, and charity – and the four cardinal virtues devised by Aristotle and taken up by the Catholic Church through Thomas Aquinas – prudence, justice, fortitude, and temperance – are from Pisano's workshop. Finally, the tower's eastern side only displays five tiles instead of seven at ground level – namely, the arts of rowing, justice, farming, theatre, and architecture – to make room for the tower's entrance, and the usual seven above them, depicting the classical arts of the *trivium* – grammar, dialectic, and rhetoric – and the *quadrivium* – arithmetic, music, geometry, and astronomy –, the *artes liberales* (liberal arts) in which classical education was rooted since Ancient Greece and Ancient Rome.

On the Campanile's third level, sixteen niches house white marble statues depicting sibyls – female prophetic figures of the Greek and Roman religions –, Biblical patriarchs, and prophets from the Old Testament. Half of them are the work of Andrea Pisano and his son Nino, sculpted in the fourteenth century; the remaining eight were created by great Renaissance master Donatello and his pupil Nanni di Bartolo in the first decades of the fifteenth century. The statue of the prophet Habacuc (nicknamed "Zuccone") and the sculptural group of Abraham and Isaac depicting the Biblical episode of the sacrifice of Isaac, both by Donatello, are the best-known ones.

The Binding of Isaac, in particular, is considered a masterpiece of Renaissance art. It was the first monumental group created in the Renaissance that was composed of two figures sculpted in a single block of marble, and the figure of Isaac was the first example of a life-size nude since ancient times. It was also the first time in the history of sculpture that a third figure – the angel – was only alluded to, by way of Abraham's tilted head, rather than being physically shown. A new relationship between form and space, figure and imagination, was thus born. The statues displayed on the tower today are copies. The originals are exhibited in the cathedral museum right behind the church – the Museo dell'Opera del Duomo –, a 65,000-square-foot (5,800-square-meter) space on three floors.

The Campanile's three upper levels were designed and built by sculptor and architect Francesco Talenti, the new project supervisor. He gave up the lavish decorations preferred by his predecessors in favor of paired mullioned windows on levels three and four, providing a vertical thrust to the tower, and a triple lancet window on level five, where the bells are housed. The tower is topped out by a vast platform from where a breathtaking view of Florence can be enjoyed. Thanks to the uniform marble cladding, the buttresses joining the different floors together, and the exquisite proportions typical of classical art, the Campanile appears as a coherent and elegant structure despite being the result of three different minds over a quarter of a century with several interruptions.

Seven working bells are at the top of the bell tower, one for each musical note. The largest and oldest one is dedicated to Santa Reparata, the ancient cathedral's titular saint. It dates to 1705 and weighs over five tons. The other six have monikers linked to the Virgin Mary, after which the new cathedral is named. They are the Apostolica, the Mater Dei, the Annunziata, the Immacolata, the Assunta, and the Misericordia. They are much younger, having been fused between 1830 (the Misericordia) and 1957 (the Apostolica). Five older bells, no longer in use, are still housed in the belfry. The bells ring different melodies depending on the changing religious holidays. The archive of the Opera di Santa Maria del Fiore (the cathedral's museum) preserves a thirteenth-century codex that is an essential guide in the knowledge of the history of the Florentine church: the *Mores et consuetudines canonice Florentine*. It also describes the various manners in which the bells would ring according to the liturgical rite of the day. Since the Middle Ages, the cathedral's Campanile was a staple in Florence's city life.

With Giotto concentrating on the bell tower, work on the cathedral languished for a while before being taken up by Andrea Pisano, who was more interested in finishing Giotto's project than completing the church. In 1348, he was killed by the infamous Black Plague that decimated Europe's population between 1346 and 1353, but work quickly resumed under Francesco Talenti, appointed in 1349, who was able to complete the bell tower and make progress on the cathedral. However, he was sacked in 1364 for allegedly not being present enough on the job site.

The cathedral was only completed much later, after the construction of Brunelleschi's dome. On 25 March 1436, Pope Eugene IV officially consecrated the church. But a key piece of this magnificent cathedral was still missing: its façade was in a provisional state, lacking most of the striking decoration every visitor marvels at today. On several occasions, Florence lords from the Medici family tried to finally get it done. First, there was an attempt by Lorenzo in 1491, whose competition to complete the façade came to nothing. Then, in 1587, it was Francesco I's turn to try to put the finishing touches on this Renaissance masterpiece, but the design by architect Bernardo Buontalenti was never realized. Only in 1871, after many discussions and an international contest, was the definitive design assigned to the Florentine architect Emilio De Fabris, who died in 1883 without seeing his project completed. At long last, it was Tuscan architect Luigi Del Moro to see through this seemingly unending task. In 1887, Florence's citizens and visitors from all over the world could gasp in admiration before this wondrous creation.

The façade's iconographic theme takes up both that of the first one by Arnolfo di Cambio, mainly dedicated to the Virgin Mary, and that of the adjoining bell tower, dominated by the topic of Christianity as the engine of the world. Just below the central rose window in the gallery, there is a Madonna with Child flanked by the statues of the twelve apostles. The tympanum of the central cusp houses a relief depicting the Assumption of Our Lady by Tuscan sculptor Augusto Passaglia. The niches of the buttresses are decorated with four statues representing – from left to right – Cardinal Pietro Valeriani, who started the construction of the cathedral in 1296; Bishop Agostino Tinacci, who blessed its foundation stones; Pope Eugene IV, who inaugurated the church in 1436; and Saint Antonino Pierozzi, Archbishop of Florence from 1446 to 1459.

Three large bronze doors punctuate the façade. The central door and the left one are by Augusto Passaglia, whereas the Florentine sculptor and painter Giuseppe Cassioli made the right one. They all date back to the period between 1899 and 1903, and are decorated with scenes from the life of the Virgin. The three lunette mosaics were realized by painter Nicolò Barabino, a Genoese artist, between 1885 and 1887. The central one shows a Christ enthroned, with Mary, Saint John Baptist, and other saints.

The cathedral's exterior walls are entirely covered in white marble plates enhanced by green marble bands, with some red accents, replicating the appearance of Giotto's Campanile and the Baptistery of St. John nearby. The northern and southern sides are basically identical and are divided into three spans. In the first span, three blinded mullioned windows on each side lighten the wall's appearance but give no light to the inside. All the light for the church's lateral naves comes from the two bigger mullioned windows on the second and third span, while the central, taller nave receives the light from eight round windows opened high above the cathedral's main body, four per side.

The apse area comprises three apses, symmetrically placed around the immense octagonal dome. They face east, south, and north and are topped by three "dead podiums" strengthened by buttresses. This was an expedient devised by Brunelleschi to provide more stability to his massive and extremely heavy dome, but they are masterpieces of Renaissance architecture in their own right. Michelangelo's *David* – arguably the most famous statue in the world – was initially bound to be displayed on one of the buttresses on the northern apse before being diverted to piazza della Signoria (then piazza dei Priori) – where it was much more accessible to the public – to do justice to its unmatched beauty and artistic importance. Nowadays, the statue standing in front of Palazzo Vecchio is a copy, as is another one in piazzale Michelangelo. The original five-ton sculpture is safely kept at the Galleria dell'Accademia Museum.

The cathedral's Gothic interior is a vast space with a strong impression of airy emptiness. In part, that's due to the austerity of religious life favored by Girolamo Savonarola, the Dominican friar who had such a strong influence over Florence's public life just in the years of the cathedral interior's fitting, both as a theologian and a politician of sorts. Additionally, many original decorations were lost over the centuries while others were relocated to the Opera del Duomo Museum, such as the magnificent choir by Donatello and Luca della Robbia – a Florentine sculptor, ceramist, and goldsmith.

The powerful Savonarola was excommunicated in 1497 by Pope Alexander VI Borgia and burned at the stake as a heretic the following year. In a twist of fate, in 1997, on the fourth centenary of his death, the General Postulation of the Dominican Order asked the Diocese of Florence to initiate a cause for beatification of the controversial character, which was approved by Cardinal Silvano Piovanelli, Archbishop of Florence. However, the Holy See never signed off on it, so nothing happened.

Simple and austere, the church's massive spans are only ten feet (three meters) lower than those of the tallest Gothic church in France, the Cathedral of Saint Peter in Beauvais, and cover an immense space with the help of very few supports. The cathedral completely lacks the "stone forest" typical of Gothic architecture, to be found north of the Alps or in churches faithful to that model, such as the Milan

Cathedral (inaugurated in 1577), meaning there is no precedent for a project of this size and structure.

The cathedral is home to the most extensive collection of stained-glass windows created in Italy in the fifteenth century. Forty-four windows in the naves and transept portray saints from the Old and New Testament, while the circular windows above the entrance and in the dome drum depict Jesus Christ and the Virgin Mary. Some of these decorations were created by the most celebrated Florentine artists of the time, such as Donatello, Lorenzo Ghiberti, Paolo Uccello, and Andrea del Castagno.

BRUNELLESCHI'S DOME

Filippo Brunelleschi was born in Florence in 1377, the son of a notary. To suit the young Filippo's artistic inclinations, his father entrusted him to a friend of his who was a goldsmith. In 1401, at the age of twenty-four, Filippo was admitted to the Silk Weavers Guild as a master goldsmith. But sculpture was his calling, and he was good enough to be allowed to participate in the contest for the design of the bronze doors of the Baptistery of St. John that same year. Victory went to Lorenzo Ghiberti, a young, up-and-coming sculptor approximately his age, but Filippo was nonetheless praised for his proposal. Today, both *Binding of Isaac* bronze groups presented by the two competitors hang side by side in the National Museum of Florence.

Shortly after that, Brunelleschi added

architecture to his passions, likely after an extended stay in Rome, where he got to know the great monuments of the Classical Era. In this field, he went on to celebrate his greatest triumph, entering history. In November 1404, he was called by the builders working on the Santa Maria del Fiore construction site to discuss some criticism leveled at the foreman Giovanni d'Ambrogio, who was directing the works at the time. This episode shows how much Brunelleschi was already keeping an eye on Florence's rising cathedral. It is believed that he shared the workers' mistrust in d'Ambrogio, who nonetheless kept his job until 1418.

On 19 August 1418, the call for tenders for the dome destined to crown the almost finished cathedral was issued, with an award of two hundred golden florins for the winner. Seventeen projects were submitted, among which the officials in charge chose those of Filippo Brunelleschi and Lorenzo Ghiberti. Both built a wooden model of their design to present in the piazza del Duomo, and they were tasked with realizing a cupola that needed to be impressive enough to become the indisputable symbol of Florence's greatness. The undertaking was herculean. A dome that massive had never been built since the Pantheon in Rome in the second century CE. The dome's octagonal drum, constructed between 1410 and 1413, was 137 feet (42 meters) wide and had walls 13 feet (4 meters) thick. No wooden scaffolding could ever support the weight of such a colossal covering, which amounts to 29,000 tons, forcing Brunelleschi to become creative.

Brunelleschi had to devise a construction system that could do without scaffolding to support the dome while in construction, a feat never before attempted. It was a new and daring enterprise, which he carried through brilliantly. Before getting to work, Brunelleschi carefully studied the Pantheon dome, trying to extract every secret he could from that ancient masterpiece. However, copying his distant colleagues' work was not an option. Like most ancient buildings, the Pantheon had a circular dome, whereas Santa Maria's dome would be octagonal. Moreover, although being the largest unreinforced concrete dome ever built, it "only" weighs about 5,000 tons, a fraction of the one in Florence.

One crucial inspiration Brunelleschi took from the Pantheon's dome was the big "eye" at its top, the only light source for that majestic building's interior. It confirmed to him that a structure of that kind could stand independently without necessarily relying on a keystone at its top to make it stable. What appears extraordinary in Brunelleschi's enterprise is how he was able to dismantle the Pantheon dome conceptually, in his mind, as one would do with a machine's mechanical parts or a clock's gears, only to conclude that he would need to do something radically different in Florence. Eventually, his construction choices testified to this. From the material used – brick masonry instead of concrete – to the geometry – an octagonal pavilion instead of a hemisphere – to the morphology – employing a double cap in place of the traditional single cap –everything in Brunelleschi's project was novel. The result was an architectural masterpiece of unprecedented scale, visible from almost anywhere in the city at the time.

Brunelleschi proposed a bold and risky solution: building two domes, with a smaller one inside the main one, with no scaffolding. The inner dome would have to support the external, main one, which would serve as a roof. The two domes would form a self-supporting structure never before conceived. At the time, the norm was to build hemispherical domes with the help of supporting beams, semi-circular frames used to hold up the entire structure during construction. The system devised by Brunelleschi consisted of a self-supporting double-shelled dome, where gigantic brick arches held the two domes together. Horizontal stone and wood rings would prevent the cupola from giving in to the lateral thrust, similarly to barrel hoops.

Brunelleschi's genius was even more evident in the arrangement of the bricks. Thanks to a building method never used before, called the herringbone technique, he created a spiral capable of providing the entire structure with the solidity it needed. To achieve his goal, Brunelleschi inserted one vertical brick for every three feet (90 centimeters) of bricks placed horizontally, thus creating the effect of a sort of bookend in a row of books. To give the mortar enough time to dry, the workers could only complete one row of bricks per week, meaning that the dome rose at a snail's pace. That is why it took sixteen years to complete, from 1420 to 1436.

Around three hundred workers were employed

at the dome's construction site, all under Brunelleschi's supervision. Almost all artisans in Florence were involved in the colossal enterprise one way or the other. Machinery of many kinds was used, some even invented or perfected by Brunelleschi himself. Transporting the material where it was needed was a challenge in itself. Sandstone blocks weighing around 1,700 pounds (770 kg) had to be lifted to over 160 feet (49 meters). One of the strongest, longest, and heaviest ropes ever manufactured was used at the site. It measured almost 600 feet (182 meters) in length and weighed 1,000 pounds (450 kg).

Among the most famous machines of the entire Renaissance was a winch operated by oxen instead of men, devised by Brunelleschi himself. This surprising piece of technology was designed to allow the oxen to always pull in the same direction while the winches' movement was reversible at the same time. The change in direction was carried out employing an endless screw with helical thread. With the help of this equipment, a single ox could lift a weight of 1,000 pounds to a height of about 200 feet (60 meters) in thirty minutes. Over twelve years, this winch was responsible for lifting an astounding 30,000 tons of building material – including marble, bricks, stone, and mortar – to the needed height.

The external dome has a dual function: on the one hand, it protects the internal dome – which constitutes the main bearing structure – from atmospheric agents; on the other, it raises the magnificence of the architectural object to unknown heights. The two domes are connected by twenty-four vertical, radially converging ribs. Eight are arranged in correspondence with the corners, while the other sixteen are divided into the width of the eight rib vaults. Connections on parallel horizontal planes, through stone blocks held together by metal brackets, are found on the second and third internal walkways. The corner ribs and the internal ones are connected by masonry arches arranged on nine parallel levels in a plane orthogonal to the dome's surface.

When the dome was completed on 30 August 1936, it still lacked a fitting culmination. A 19-foot-wide (6-meter) round hole needed to be sealed with something as stunning as the rest of the construction. Instead of simply commissioning the project to Brunelleschi, a new competition was organized. Unsurprisingly, Brunelleschi again emerged victorious. He designed a 68-foot-tall (21-meter) lantern to be installed at the dome's summit. Work on the lantern only started ten years later, just before Brunelleschi's death. Four successive architects thus carried out the project, and the lantern was inaugurated on 23 April 1461, though the bronze sphere with a cross at its very top by Andrea del Verrocchio was only added in 1472. With a weight of about 750 tons, the lantern has a crucial function for the dome's statics, acting as a blockage against the inward pressure generated by the cupola's immense weight. For a breathtaking view of Florence, climbing 463 steps on narrow stairs will bring you to the terrace at the lantern's base.

Climbing the cupola also allows visitors to get a close-up view of its interior decoration, which is no less impressive than its outer appearance. Initially, a mosaic decoration had been proposed, but the idea was abandoned due to concerns about the added weight this would have meant for the already colossal structure. In 1572, Grand Duke Cosimo I de' Medici instructed Giorgio Vasari – one of the best-known painters of his time – to paint the entire ceiling based on the Last Judgement subject. Both the grand duke and Vasari died in 1574, leaving the completion of the cycle of frescos to painter Federico Zuccari from the Marche region, appointed by Cosimo's son Francis. The 38,750-square-foot (3,500-square-meter) pictorial series features more than 700 painted figures. Among them are 248 angels, 235 human souls, 102 religious characters, 35 damned, and 14 monsters, together with animals, portraits, and cherubs. On 19 August 1579, this glorious masterpiece of Renaissance art was unveiled in all its splendor to the people of Florence.

BAPTISTERY OF
SAINT JOHN

The Baptistery of St. John, right in front of the cathedral, predates it by about four centuries in its
current form. It is the only Florentine church that
survived in its original shape from the times in
which Dante Alighieri – Italy's most famous and
revered poet – lived, from the late thirteenth to the
early fourteenth century. The current church is
likely the result of an expansion of an ancient Roman temple dedicated to the god Mars, dating to the
fourth century CE. It is considered a masterpiece of
Italian Romanesque style. Pope Nicholas II consecrated the Baptistery in 1059. To this day, it has the
dignity of a minor basilica in the Catholic Church.

Dante Alighieri, widely regarded as the father of
the Italian language, was baptized here. He later
honored the place in his world-famous *Divine Comedy*, the greatest masterpiece of Italian literature

ever. A memorial stone dedicated to the man Italians call "il sommo poeta"– "the Supreme Poet" – is at the Baptistery's foot. Not far from it, a second plaque proclaims Dante's wish to return to this place dear to him to receive the poetic crowning, a symbolic ceremony consecrating a poet laureate to the fame of posterity.

For several centuries, the Baptistery served as a reference model for many Florentine architects, who, after studying it thoroughly, elected it as an exemplar of ideal architecture. Florence's citizens, meanwhile, made it the city's most important public building. In 1128, it became the official baptismal font, which hosted every kind of liturgical celebration besides christening ceremonies, including major religious events. But the people of Florence also used its spaces as an elegant, covered plaza to meet, converse, or exchange political opinions.

The building has an octagonal plan, typical of late-ancient and Byzantine traditions, with a diameter of 84 feet (25.6 meters), slightly less than half of Brunelleschi's cupola. It is closed by a segmented dome invisible from the outside since it is covered by an attic topped by a pyramid roof. Each façade is divided into three horizontal levels. The lowest one features a large door on three of the eight sides; the middle has alternating arched and rectangular windows, three per side; the third and uppermost level is decorated with Corinthian pilasters. The buttresses decorated with white and green horizontal bands at the building's corners are probably from a later period.

The Baptistery's exterior is completely covered in white Carrara marble and green Prato marble. The big arches on the façades have no load-bearing function since the dome's weight is entirely supported by the exterior walls, which are as strong as they look slender. The stepped base on which the Baptistery was built cannot be seen anymore due to the gradual raising of the square's floor over the centuries. The project's classicism is apparent in its balance and harmony, but its forms are not strictly classical. Florentine Romanesque certainly took inspiration from classical architecture, but without following that model to the letter.

The Baptistery is also famous for its three beautiful bronze doors, considered masterpieces of Italian Gothic and Renaissance sculpture. The Porta Sud – southern door – is the oldest. It was commissioned by the Guild of Calimala (i.e., the merchant's guild, the most influential in Florence), who were responsible for the maintenance of the Baptistery. It was cast between 1330 and 1336 by Giotto's pupil Andrea Pisano. Its twenty-eight panels tell episodes from St. John the Baptist's life. The second door to be created was the Porta Nord – northern door – which was cast between 1401 and 1424 by Lorenzo Ghiberti and features twenty-eight panels depicting stories from the New Testament, with the four evangelists and Jesus Christ. Perhaps the most famous of the three is the Porta del Paradiso – the door of paradise – which was given its name by none other than Michelangelo, who judged the work by Lorenzo Ghiberti good enough to be used as the doors to heaven.

In this case, we are looking at ten larger panels in gilded bronze featuring stories from the Old Testament. The door was cast between 1425 and 1452.

All three of the Baptistery's doors are copies. The originals can be seen at the Opera del Duomo Museum.

The church's interior is a triumph of gold leaf mosaics, authentic masterpieces of Gothic art. The oldest ones can be found on the vault of the *scarsella*, the rectangular apse protruding from the main building. They were made by Fra' Jacopo, a Franciscan friar, starting in 1225. They depict the *Agnus Dei* (one name for Jesus Christ) surrounded by a *Madonna* and *Apostles and Prophets*, with additionally *St. John enthroned* on the left side, and a *Madonna and Child enthroned* on the right.

The dome's vault is decorated with four – partly five – concentric circles packed with figures. The uppermost circle, just below the cupola's hole, depicts the angelic hierarchies. Further down, three of the eight segments forming the dome are dedicated to a grand representation of the Last Judgement, with a large figure of Jesus at the center giving his verdict about people's sins. At his feet stand those admitted to heaven – symbolized by his right hand's palm turned upwards – and those who shall suffer in hell – as indicated by his left hand's palm turned downwards. Christ the Judge is flanked by the Virgin Mary, St. John the Baptist, and the twelve apostles. The rest of the vault is dedicated to stories from Genesis and episodes from Jesus's, Joseph's, Mary's, and St. John's lives. Several artists, including painters Cimabue and Coppo di Marcovaldo, contributed to this stunning masterwork. Decorating the dome was an expensive and long-running endeavor that lasted at least thirty years, from the early 1270s to the first years of the fourteenth century. The Baptistery's *Last Judgement* was the largest and most significant ever realized up to that day.

The flooring in the Baptistery is equally impressive and is decorated with polychrome marble inlays depicting imaginary animals and classic fabric designs inspired by a fantastical Orient. The neo-Romanesque main altar is a work by twentieth-century architect Giuseppe Castellucci, who incorporated some original fragments into its design. The baptismal font dates to 1371 and is attributed to a follower of Andrea Pisano. The pair of stoups likely comes from a follower of Arnolfo di Cambio. In front of the altar, a grate allows a glimpse of the basement housing the excavations of the ancient Roman building on which the Baptistery stands, with its geometric mosaic floors.

PIAZZA DELLA SIGNORIA
PALAZZO VECCHIO

Signoria Square, a few steps south of the city's cathedral, has been at the heart of Florence's political life for over seven centuries. Palazzo Vecchio –
the Old Palace – dates to the very beginning of the
fourteenth century, when it was built as the seat of
the Signoria, the Republic of Florence's city council
headed by the Priors, hence called Palazzo dei Priori
– the Palace of the Priors. Today, it is the city's town
hall and a museum. Over the centuries, many conse-
quential events have involved this square. On 7 February 1497, for instance, in this square, the
influential Dominican friar Girolamo Savonarola
staged the infamous "Bonfire of the Vanities," where
thousands of allegedly sinful items were burned as a
purification ritual, including numerous books and
paintings. Ironically, Savonarola himself suffered
the same fate only fifteen months later. After being
condemned for heresy, he was first hanged and then

burned at the stake in this very square. A marble plaque in front of the Fountain of Neptune recalls those events.

When, in 1299, Florence's most influential citizens decided to build a new, imposing palace that would serve as a worthy seat of the Republic's government, capable of embodying the Tuscan city's power and prestige, they entrusted the project to Arnolfo di Cambio, who was already working on the Cathedral of Santa Maria del Fiore and the Basilica of Santa Croce (Basilica of the Holy Cross). The new palace was erected upon the remains of two pre-existing buildings. In the palace's underground level, it is even possible to see the remains of the Roman Theatre of Florentia from the first century CE that stood here. Although the first iteration of the palace was ready by 1314, it took until the late sixteenth century, after several interventions, to get to its current appearance.

The most substantial renovations date to between 1342 and 1343, when Gualtieri VI of Brienne was Governor of Florence, appointed by the city's notables who wished a foreigner to rule the Republic after over one century of a grueling struggle between Guelfs and Ghibellines. Gualtieri made the palace much bigger and made it look like a fortress. Later, between 1440 and 1460, the city's undeclared ruler Cosimo de' Medici, "the Elder," requested improvements to the palace's interior, which gained an abundance of Renaissance decorations and a courtyard by famed sculptor and architect Michelozzo. The Hall of the Five Hundred, the palace's largest and most significant room, was created between 1495 and 1496 by Simone del Pollaiolo and Francesco di Domenico on commission from Girolamo Savonarola, at the time the *de facto* ruler of Florence.

The building was renamed Palazzo Ducale – Duke's Palace – in 1540, when Grand Duke Cosimo I de' Medici made it his residence, only to receive its definitive name of Palazzo Vecchio in 1587 when Grand Duke Francis de' Medici moved to Palazzo Pitti, another of Florence's impressive Renaissance mansions. Both buildings were connected by an elevated and covered passageway – the Vasari Corridor – built to a design by architect Giorgio Vasari, which crosses the Arno River over the Ponte Vecchio, the city's best-known and most-visited bridge. Inside Palazzo Vecchio, several secret passageways bear witness to the Medici's constant fear of attempts on their lives by political rivals, which were never lacking in Florence.

The building's façade is dominated by the Torre di Arnolfo (Arnolfo's Tower), named after Arnolfo di Cambio and erected around 1310. It is just short of 310 feet (94 meters) tall and stands to the right of the façade's center since it was built taking advantage of a preexistent tower incorporated into Palazzo Vecchio, as shown by the walled-up windows. Inside the tower, a small room called Alberghetto served as a prison cell for Cosimo de' Medici the Elder before he was sentenced to exile in 1433 and Girolamo Savonarola while waiting to be executed in May 1498.

A series of coats of arms decorates the highest part of the façade, just under the arches of the overhanging gallery. There are nine, repeated twice, each representing some part of the city's history and politics. From left to right, the first one is the Cross of the People, a red cross on a silver shield adopted in 1292 as the emblem of the Florentine people. Then comes Florence's official coat of arms, the red lily on a silver shield, followed by a shield divided into two halves, one red and one white, which symbolizes the union between Florence and Fiesole in 1125 and is now the crest of Florence's municipality. The red shield with a pair of golden keys is the banner of the Catholic Church, symbolizing the alliance with the Republic in its fight against the Ghibellines.

The fifth shield is blue and shows the writing LIBERTAS – freedom – in golden letters. It was chosen by the Republic as its coat of arms when it gained its independence from the empire. The next coat of arms, a red eagle stomping on a green dragon, was assigned to the Florentines by Pope Clemens IV when they helped his party against King Manfred of Sicily – a Ghibelline – in 1265. The seventh shield is Florence's ancient coat of arms – the silver (or white) lily on a red background – before the colors were inverted. It is followed by the coat of arms that Charles of Anjou assigned the city as a sign of gratitude for helping him defeat Manfred of Sicily. It is made of many small golden lilies on a blue background. The ninth and last emblem is the coat of arms of King Robert of Naples, also an Anjou, who governed Florence from 1313 to 1318 at the invitation of the city's notables. All these coats of arms were painted in 1343 and restored in 1792, after they were worn by time.

The rest of the square is famous for its statues and the Fountain of Neptune, the Roman god of the sea inspired by his Greek counterpart Poseidon. Situated at Palazzo Vecchio's northwestern corner, this fountain was commissioned in 1550 by Cosimo I de' Medici. This area of the city had always had water supply problems, and Cosimo, who lived in the Palazzo with his whole family, thought he could kill two birds with one stone. The fountain would solve his drinking water issues while, at the same time, being a self-celebratory monument thanks to the giant statue of Neptune that would decorate it. To this aim, sculptor Bartolomeo Ammannati gave the sea god an unmistakable resemblance to the duke himself. Due to the statue's immaculate whiteness, derived from the white Carrara marble it is made of, the Florentines were quick to nickname it "Il Biancone," which can be translated as "The Very White."

The fountain, with all its bronze and marble sculptural groups, was completed in 1575. Its octagonal basin contains the four horses of Neptune's chariot – two are done in white marble, and two are pinkish – whose wheels are decorated with the zodiac signs, symbolizing the passage of time. Four bronze sculptured groups decorate the basin's perimeter, each depicting a marine divinity – the bearded god Nereus; his wife Doris, with whom he fathered the Nereids; the goddess Thetis, the most beautiful among the Nereids and mother of the

Homeric hero Achilles; and Oceanus, Thetis's brother, through whom all water is generated – accompanied by a procession of satyrs and nymphs.

Neptune's statue – over 18 feet (5.6 meters) tall – faced a somewhat "unfair" competition. Just a few steps away stood the *David* by Michelangelo, perhaps the greatest artist that ever lived. The undisputed master of the Italian Renaissance had created his masterpiece, universally considered one of the most beautiful sculptures in the history of art, between 1501 and 1504. Initially destined for one of the cathedral's buttresses as a decoration, once completed, it became apparent that it was way too significant to be put in such a secluded location. After a lengthy discussion – in which the likes of Leonardo da Vinci, Sandro Botticelli, Andrea Sansovino, and others participated – the most obvious choice was made, and the statue had found its rightful place in Florence's most important square.

There is a second statue in the square with Cosimo I's features. It is his bronze equestrian monument, immediately to the north of Palazzo Vecchio and looking west. Cosimo's son Francesco I commissioned it in 1587 to Giambologna – a moniker given to the Flemish sculptor Jean de Boulogne, who was very active in Florence – to celebrate his father's role as the first officially recognized Grand Duke of Tuscany. It took the foreign artist twelve years to complete the monument, including a series of bas-reliefs decorating its base, which depict the feats of Cosimo's life. Giambologna's work was so well received that he was tasked with realizing also another important equestrian monument in Florence. Ferdinando I de' Medici, who had become Grand Duke after the unexpected death of his brother Francesco, asked Giambologna to create also his own bronze equestrian statue, which was finished in 1607 and placed in piazza della Santissima Annunziata in October 1608, only four months before Ferdinando's passing. The statue was cast with bronze coming from the cannons of Turkish galleys defeated by the Order of Saint Stephen – created by Cosimo I – in the sixteenth century.

Two very different statues frame Palazzo Vecchio's main entrance: Michelangelo's *David* on the left and *Hercules and Cacus* on the right. The *David* is widely recognized as one of the world's most important works of art and the perfect ideal of male beauty. It is 17 feet (5.2 meters) tall, including its base, and depicts the Biblical hero and future second King of Israel just before facing Goliath, the Philistine giant he will kill with a slingshot throw. The sculpture in piazza della Signoria is a copy; the original, too fragile and precious to be kept outside, can be seen in the Galleria dell'Accademia Museum.

The *Hercules and Cacus* group is a work by Florentine sculptor Bartolomeo Brandini – who went by the name Baccio Bandinelli – who was called to replace Michelangelo because of the latter's commitments in Rome at the pope's court (the Sixtine Chapel in the Vatican City among them). The allegorical theme of this sculpture in white marble – completed in 1534 – is that of the demi-god Hercules' strength and ingenuity defeating the wickedness of Cacus, a fire-belching monster from Greek and Roman mythology. The depiction of this episode narrated by Virgil and other poets in the *Twelve Labors of Hercules* saga served to celebrate the triumph of the Medici family (Hercules) over the Republicans (represented by Cacus). From an artistic perspective, Bandinelli's work has attracted much criticism from the very beginning. It was judged as a poor attempt by the lesser artist to equal the perfection of Michelangelo's *David*, with an unsatisfactory outcome. The entire sculptural group is permeated with not-so-subtle gigantism, and its display of muscularity does not translate into expressiveness and dynamic thrust.

Finally, to the right of Palazzo Vecchio is a kind of open-air art gallery in the form of a portico called Loggia dei Lanzi (or Loggia della Signoria). Inaugurated in 1381, this is where many of the Republic's ceremonies and public assemblies took place. It got its name from the lansquenets, the feared German mercenaries in Emperor Charles V's service, who are said to have camped out under its arches on their way to Rome in 1527. The Loggia houses several statues from the Roman era and some masterpieces from the sixteenth century. The most important ones are *The Rape of the Sabines* by Giambologna, completed around 1580, and *Perseus holding the head of Medusa*, a 17-foot-tall (5.2 meters) bronze statue by famed goldsmith and sculptor Benvenuto Cellini completed in 1554, which was meant not only as a work of art but also as a warning to the Medici dynasty's enemies, represented by the severed head of the Medusa. Right behind this Gothic masterpiece lies the Galleria degli Uffizi, Florence's most famous museum and the most visited in the country.

The Feldherrnhalle in Munich, Germany, was built in the nineteenth century on the model of the Loggia.

PONTE VECCHIO

Ponte Vecchio – the "Old Bridge" – is far and away the best-known and most visited of the dozen bridges crossing the Arno River in the city's territory. The bridge was built where an ancient Roman wooden footbridge stood, built perhaps in the first century BCE when the city was still known as Florentia. It is the oldest bridge still standing in a city that has seen countless river crossings destroyed by the force of the Arno's turbulent waters. The first Ponte Vecchio dates to the years after 1177 when it had to be rebuilt following its predecessor's collapse in one of the river's frequent floods. This iteration was built in stone and wood and survived floods – in 1200, 1250, 1269, and 1288 – and fires – in 1222, 1322, and 1331 – before succumbing to a massive flood that destroyed every bridge in Florence, on 4 November 1333.

It is disputed which architect designed the

current bridge between 1339 and 1345. According to Giorgio Vasari, an architect and painter and the most highly regarded art historian of the Italian Renaissance, there was the hand of Taddeo Gaddi, a pupil of Giotto. Whoever was responsible for the project did a great job, so much so that the newly constructed bridge withstood the elements and the river's bad temper to this day. It was erected in pietraforte – a typical stone from the area – and is supported by only three arches separated by two slender and perfectly shaped piles. At the time, Ponte Vecchio linked Florence proper – first and foremost, the area around Piazza della Signoria – to the outer district across the river, known as Oltrarno ("beyond the Arno").

Over the centuries, the bridge's appearance has changed considerably. Originally, forty-three small shops were housed in four rectangular buildings – two on each side of the bridge – separated by a small court in the bridge's center. Like every other bridge at that time, Ponte Vecchio must have had its dedicated chapel, most likely similar to the Rucellai Chapel, which can be visited in the Church of San Pancrazio (Saint Pancras), nowadays a museum. For a century and a half, all shops on the bridge belonged to the Municipality of Florence, which received significant rent revenue. Most shops were occupied by Florence's greengrocers and butchers, whose malodorous and blood-dripping carts were not welcome in the patrician part of town.

In 1495, the municipality sold all shops to private retailers and institutions, both secular and religious.

Slowly but surely, the new owners radically changed Ponte Vecchio's look by adding multi-story cantilevered volumes overlooking the river below on both sides of the bridge. The original design's symmetries, balance, and unity were lost forever, and the bridge acquired that characteristic aesthetics for which it is known today. In 1565, Cosimo I commissioned what would be known as the Vasari Corridor to connect the city's political and administrative center to his private residence south of the river, the majestic Palazzo Pitti. One side of the bridge's central court was thus closed by a three-arched portico that supports a section of said corridor.

Cosimo's son and heir, Ferdinand I, was not happy with the mixture of butchers, grocers, cobblers, woodcutters, and many other businesses populating the bridge at the time. He despised the stench, chaos, and vulgarity emanating from those shops, which he witnessed from above when crossing the Vasari Corridor. So, in 1593, he ordered the eviction of all "indecorous" activities and ordered all shops to be assigned exclusively to goldsmiths, silversmiths, and jewelers. Thus, the modern Ponte Vecchio was born with its gold, silver, and diamond feast. A place, in Ferdinand's words, "very popular with gentlemen and foreigners." As a matter of fact, customers and sightseers from all over Europe began flocking to Ponte Vecchio.

In November 1844, there was a terrible flood, but the bridge again withstood the river's fury. In 1901, a bust of Benvenuto Cellini – considered the "Prince of Goldsmiths" – was erected in the open tract of the central court. Overlooking it are three large rectangular windows in the Vasari corridor, which were built on the orders of Italy's Fascist Duce Benito Mussolini on the occasion of Nazi Germany's Adolf Hitler's visit to Florence on 9 May 1938. Mussolini was keen on offering his august guest the best possible panoramic view of the city. Six years later, in the summer of 1944, it was Germany's consul in Florence – Gerhard Wolf – to save Ponte Vecchio from the Nazis' destructive rampage when the retreating German army blew up all other bridges on the Arno River. A commemorative plaque on the eastern side of the bridge honors Wolf's act of bravery, for which the Florentines are forever grateful.

Ponte Vecchio is listed among Italy's officially recognized national monuments.

CHURCHES

Like every other Italian town, Florence is a city of Catholic churches. At least six – besides Santa Maria del Fiore and the Baptistery of St. John – need mentioning.

Santa Maria Novella

Santa Maria Novella is Florence's main train station. If you come by train, you will most likely arrive at this station. More alluring, though, is the namesake basilica a few steps away from the station entrance. It has always been the heart of the Dominican Order in town since its inception. Before it was built, in its place, there was the small church of Santa Maria delle Vigne – Saint Mary of the Vineyards –dating to 1094 and so-named because it was originally located on the city's outskirts, surrounded by vineyards. In 1221, the church was transferred to the Dominican community in Florence, which soon resolved they needed a much bigger and more prestigious house of worship.

The new church was consecrated in 1420 but only received its finishing touches in 1920 when the marble façade was finally completed. Realized in several successive steps, the building shows the participation of many architects, both in its interior and outside. With construction starting in the second half of the thirteenth century, the original design was Gothic but was later heavily modified in Renaissance style. It is believed that the façade's lower part in white and green marble – with a touch of red above the main entrance – is due to fra (brother) Jacopo Talenti of the Dominican Order, who realized it around 1350 thanks to a generous donation from one Turino del Baldese. The two lateral Gothic portals were created at this time.

In 1439, Pope Eugene IV stayed at the convent attached to the church during the influential Council of Florence, which sought to reunite the Greek (Eastern) and Latin (Western) Churches, but the church's façade was only half done. The Dominican friars had to wait another twenty years before the wealthy Florentine merchant Giovanni Rucellai provided the necessary funding. Architect Leon Battista Alberti thus completed the façade's beautiful superior section. Alberti, a shining example of the humanist movement as a writer, mathematician, linguist, musicologist, and philosopher, was also responsible for the main portal in classical style, inspired by the Pantheon in Rome. Above it, the full-width trabeation features a geometric decoration representing a sail in the wind, the emblem of the Rucellai family. On the architrave high up, an inscription remembers the benefactor with these words: IOHA(N) NES ORICELLARIUS PAV(LI) F(ILIUS) AN(NO) SAL(VTIS) MCDLXX, which means "Giovanni Rucellai, son of Paolo, the year 1470."

The basilica's interior welcomes visitors with a wealth of artistic treasures. Among them are frescos by Domenico Bigordi, known as Ghirlandaio – one of Florence Renaissance's most appreciated painters at the time of Lorenzo the Magnificent –, Filippino Lippi, and Andrea Orcagna. Other masterpieces include a stunning crucifix by a young Giotto – a 19-foot-tall (5.80 meters) work done in tempera and gold – and a remarkable fresco of the Divine Trinity by Tommaso di ser Giovanni di Mone di Andreuccio, known as Masaccio, a painter instrumental in changing the history of art in Florence by rejecting the decorative excesses typical of the late Gothic style most used at the time. The polychrome windows, dating to 1492, are the work of one Alessandro Agolanti but are based on a design by Ghirlandaio.

Inside the basilica, several lateral chapels are full of Renaissance marvels, too. There is, for instance, the Strozzi Chapel with the impressive fresco cycle by Filippino Lippi – a pupil of Botticelli's – featuring stories from the lives of St. Philip the Apostle and St. John the Evangelist. Or the Gondi Chapel to the left of the main chapel, where a crucifix by Filippo Brunelleschi – the only known wooden sculpture by the great artist – hangs. The church is also home to paintings and frescos by Bronzino, one of Florence Renaissance's most skilled portraitists, and his pupil Alessandro Allori. And the list goes on.

Annexed to the basilica is the Dominican convent – now mainly a museum – with three beautiful cloisters and a refectory full of exciting pieces and works of art.

Santa Croce

The Basilica di Santa Croce – Basilica of the Holy Cross – is one of Italy's most significant examples of Gothic architecture. It has the rank of a minor basilica (just as Santa Maria Novella) and is an Italian national monument. The first stone was laid in 1294, and this beautiful church was consecrated in 1443. During its centuries-old history, at least four popes visited the basilica: Eugene IV, Sixtus IV, Leo X, and Clement XIV. Before that, the old, much smaller church of Santa Croce had seen prominent religious figures such as Saint Anthony of Padua (Portuguese by birth), Saint Bonaventure – professor at the Sorbonne in Paris, friends with St. Thomas Aquinas, Minister General of the Franciscan Order, and proclaimed a Doctor of the Church by Pope Sixtus V in 1588 –, and Saint Louis of Anjou, a prince of the Neapolitan royal house of Anjou.

The basilica was built somewhat to the southeast of Santa Maria del Fiore, much nearer to the river, in an area that was marshland subject to frequent flooding at the time. According to tradition, the first group of Franciscan friars arrived in Florence around 1209 – St. Francis himself visited in 1211 – and settled among the villagers outside the city walls. When Francis of Assisi was proclaimed a saint by Pope Gregory IX in 1228, only two years after his death, the first church of Santa Croce was already standing. By 1267, that building had been replaced by a bigger one, but the ever-growing influx of believers forced the Franciscan Order to take more radical measures. Hence, the project of a monumental church was born: the current Basilica of Santa Croce.

Arnolfo di Cambio, perhaps the most respected Florentine architect and sculptor of the time, was entrusted with the project. When he died around 1310, the apse was almost done. The transept was then built, followed by the naves. By 1385, the church was completed. The sheer amount of great art decorating the church's interior makes it impossible to compile a list here. Suffice it to say that the famous *Stendhal syndrome* – a psycho-somatic disorder manifesting itself with a feeling of widespread malaise associated with psychic and physical symptoms in front of works of art or architecture of incomparable beauty, primarily if they are found in limited spaces – is named after the description famed nineteenth-century French author Marie-Henri Beyle, simply known as Stendhal, made of his overwhelming feelings during a visit to Santa Croce:

"I had reached that level of emotion where the celestial sensations given by the arts and

passionate feelings meet. Leaving Santa Croce, I had a heartbeat; life had dried up for me, I walked fearing I would fall." Stendhal described better than anyone else the feeling of loss felt after a visit to Santa Croce, testifying to the extraordinary richness and uniqueness of the artistic heritage preserved inside the basilica.

Most masterpieces can be seen in the side chapels, like the Peruzzi Chapel and the Bardi Chapel on the right, both frescoed by Giotto with stories of St. John the Baptist, St. John the Evangelist, and St. Francis. All painted by the great master in his late years, these works are considered Giotto's artistic testament and greatly influenced the subsequent generation of Florentine painters, Ghirlandaio being one obvious example. Another peculiarity of Santa Croce is that it is home to over three hundred tombs, often of famous people of the past. Michelangelo Buonarroti, Niccolò Machiavelli, Galileo Galilei, Leon Battista Alberti, composer Giocacchino Rossini, and writer and poet Ugo Foscolo are all buried here, together with countless others. Two hundred seventy-six marble slabs on the basilica's floor represent as many tombs, and many more can be found on the walls between the altars. A spectacular tomb had been readied for Dante Alighieri as well, but Florence could never convince the city of Ravenna to hand over the remains of this giant of Italian language and poetry.

Michelangelo's monumental tomb is truly magnificent and full of symbolism. Designed by Giorgio Vasari, it is decorated with marble statues of three afflicted figures symbolizing painting, sculpture, and architecture. Michelangelo's state funeral, on 14 July 1564, was more typical for a prince than an artist. It was also the definitive consecration of a man who had reached unsurpassed creative highs in every artistic field in which he had tried his hand.

Another artistic jewel lies on the basilica's right, at the end of the cloister. It is the Pazzi Chapel, a masterpiece by Filippo Brunelleschi – the creator of the world-famous dome of Santa Maria del Fiore, Florence's most recognizable landmark – built between 1442 and 1478. Andrea de' Pazzi commissioned the chapel as a private memorial chapel for the family, although it was also used as the Franciscan chapter house. After a major fire had destroyed the area of the dormitory and part of the library in 1423, the Pazzi family – one of the city's wealthiest – seized the opportunity to build a monument to themselves by offering to pay for it. Brunelleschi was involved in the project until he died in 1446. Completing the chapel took another thirty years before all members of the Pazzi family were either killed or banished from Florence in the wake of the ill-fated conspiracy to overthrow the Medici rule over the city (see chapter History).

Santa Maria del Carmine

Completely different in its outward appearance is the Basilica of Santa Maria del Carmine – St. Mary of the Mount Carmel – located in Oltrarno, i.e., south of the river. This is because the façade has never been completed in the Gothic style – rich in white and green marble – typical of other notable churches in town, leaving the stone and brick of the original façade exposed. Construction began in 1268 upon the initiative of a group of Carmelite friars from Pisa. The church was completed in 1475, but it had to be entirely rebuilt after a terrible fire destroyed it almost completely in 1771. That is why, on the inside, almost everything dates to the eighteenth century, except several paintings from the sixteenth and seventeenth centuries.

The basilica's claim to fame is the much-admired Brancacci Chapel, one of Florence's greatest artistic treasures, which thankfully was spared by the flames when the rest of the church burned down. The Brancacci, an ancient patrician family, always owned the chapel at the head of the church's transept. In 1423, after his return from an embassy in Egypt, Felice Brancacci commissioned the chapel's decoration to the Aretine painter Masaccio – one of Renaissance's initiators – and his mentor Masolino da Panicale. Sadly, Masaccio died unexpectedly in 1428, at only twenty-seven years of age, leaving the decoration unfinished. The missing parts were completed between 1481 and 1483 by Filippino Lippi. The chapel's stunning fresco cycle depicts a *historia salutis* – i.e., the traditional history of man's salvation from Adam to St. Peter as the direct heir of Jesus Christ and founder of the Roman Church – with scenes from Genesis, the Gospels, the Book of Acts, and the Golden Legend by Jacopo da Varazze, a medieval collection of hagiographic biographies.

The chapel is dedicated to St. Peter, the Catholic Church's first pope, whom Pietro Brancacci, the family's founder, considered his protector.

Santo Spirito

Just a few steps from Santa Maria del Carmine stands another of Florence's most notable churches, the Basilica di Santo Spirito (Basilica of the Holy Ghost), built on the ruins of a thirteenth-century Augustinian convent. Its story started in 1250 when two Florentines gifted an Augustinian friar a simple house with a piece of vineyard on the southern bank of the Arno, where the first group of friars built their first church and convent. This complex quickly became a significant cultural, artistic, and theological center. Its library was well known to intellectuals like Francesco Petrarca, who, thanks to it, got acquainted with the thought of St. Augustin and even used the Doctor of the Church's *Confessions* as an inspiration for his work in Latin prose *Secretum*. Giovanni Boccaccio frequented the convent, too.

The current basilica, built between 1444 and 1487, has a very plain exterior architecture. It lacks a spectacular façade like those of its siblings in Florence and is devoid of most of the rich decoration typical of the city's other prominent basilicas. Which doesn't mean a lesser architect designed it. In fact, none other than Filippo Brunelleschi was involved in the project until he died in 1446. Still, its actual calling card lies in its interior. There, Santo Spirito offers an itinerary of beauty resulting from the work of some of Florence's most talented artists. Upon entering the basilica, the perfectly balanced Renaissance architecture, its sandstone columns with Corinthian capitals, and its harmonious perspective regale the visitor with a feeling of freedom and space. With its Baroque ciborium, the main altar is a sight to behold.

Among the most precious masterpieces hosted inside the church is a wooden crucifix that a young Michelangelo made as a thank-you to the prior of Santo Spirito for his hospitality and the opportunity to study anatomy. Other notable works of art include an *Annunciation* by Pietro del Donzello, an altarpiece by Filippino Lippi adorning the altar of the Nerli family (the Pala Nerli), and a copy of Michelangelo's *Pietà* – the one displayed in St. Peter's Basilica in Rome – by Nanni di Baccio Bigio.

San Lorenzo

Back to the inner city, just north of Santa Maria del Fiore, the Basilica of San Lorenzo (Saint Lawrence) is built on the site of the oldest church in town. That one was consecrated in 392 CE to Saint Lawrence – the Christian martyr Laurentius, who was put to death in Rome in 258 during the persecution ordered by Emperor Valerian – by Saint Ambrose, the Bishop of Milan who played a crucial role in winning the Church a level of independence from the Empire not previously seen. The ancient church was consecrated anew in 1095 after enlargement works commissioned by Pope Nicholas II, who had been Bishop of Florence.

The current appearance and architectural layout are the work of Filippo Brunelleschi. The entire complex, which comprises the basilica itself, the Laurentian Library, and the Medici Chapels, is considered a masterpiece of the Renaissance. The sacristy was completed in 1428, in time to host Giovanni de' Medici's solemn funeral ceremony in 1429, but the reconstruction works of the entire church progressed only slowly. After 1441, the site supervision was taken over by architect and sculptor Michelozzo – Michele di Bartolomeo Michelozzi – who also created the splendid Palazzo Medici Riccardi for Cosimo de' Medici (the Elder). Brunelleschi, by then, was old and busy with other projects.

The church's façade is very obviously unfinished. In 1516, Pope Leo X – himself a Medici – commissioned Michelangelo to design an apt frontage for such an important place of worship, but the project was abandoned due to financial and practical difficulties. A wooden model of Michelangelo's design – measuring 85 by 111 inches (2.16 by 2.83 meters) – can be seen at the great artist's museum house, Casa Buonarroti, where the Renaissance's undisputed genius used to live. The annexed library – the Biblioteca Medicea Laurenziana – was also designed by Michelangelo.

The basilica's main altar was consecrated in 1461. Cosimo, who died three years later, was buried in an underground crypt exactly beneath it, starting a tradition that lasted until the eighteenth century. The tombs of most members of the Medici family can be found in this church and the adjacent Medici Chapels, now a museum with access from piazza Madonna degli Aldobrandini. The Chapels are considered a self-celebration of Florence's most influential family throughout three centuries. Work on the mausoleum was started in 1520 when Cardinal Giulio de' Medici – who would later be pope with the name of Clement VII – commissioned Michelangelo to realize a space vast and sumptuous enough to receive the mortal remains of all members of the Medici House in a manner worthy of their rank. By 1533, Michelangelo completed the New Sacristy before moving to Rome to work for Pope Clement VII and Pope Paul III. Still, the work on other parts of the Chapels lasted until one century later. The Cappella dei Principi – Chapel of the Princes – boasts the second most majestic dome in town after that by Brunelleschi atop he cathedral, being 193 feet (59 meters) tall.

San Miniato al Monte

San Miniato is an abbey basilica with the status of a minor basilica. It is called "al Monte" – "at the Mount" – because of its location high on a hill south of the river from where visitors can enjoy a beautiful view over most of the city. It is one of five abbeys founded in and around Florence. At its main entrance, a marble inscription reminds visitors that HAEC EST PORTA COELI – "this is the gate of heaven" –, Jacob's famous exclamation after he dreamed of a ladder whose top reached the sky, with angels climbing and descending it (Genesis 28,17). So, this is how Florentines imagined paradise in the eleventh century!

Saint Miniato was said to be either a Greek merchant or an Armenian prince who settled in Florence – then Florentia – to live as a hermit. He died a martyr, beheaded during Decius' persecution. First a sanctuary and later a small chapel rose on the site of his hermitage, where the current basilica, whose construction began in 1018, now stands. The abbey was founded by Benedictine monks, whose Olivetan Congregation still inhabits it.

San Miniato's façade is one of the masterpieces of Florentine Romanesque architecture, featuring a geometric classicism inspired by the marble inlays of Rome's monumental buildings. It served as a model for the façades of Santa Maria Novella and Santa Croce, built more than two centuries later. The beautiful façade is divided into two orders, of which the lower one features five semicircular arches, a motif recurring in the church's pediment. In the upper half, the white marble with green inlays emulates the *opus reticulatum*, a Roman construction technique employing diamond-shaped pieces of tuff placed within a concrete core.

The polychrome of the exterior continues in the interior space with three naves. The church's presbytery and choir are raised above the crypt, divided into seven naves by columns recovered from buildings of the Roman era. The basilica's titular saint rests on a Romanesque altar. As is customary, there are several lateral chapels inside, and a variety of beautiful frescos decorate the ceiling and walls. There is the hand of Michelozzo and Luca della Robbia in some of the artwork. The late Byzantine apsidal mosaic above the main altar shows a scene where Saint Miniato, on the right, hands over the earthly crown to Christ Pantocrator – "ruler of all," i.e., almighty – to receive that of celestial glory in return.

Adjacent to the basilica is the monastery, and defensive walls surround the entire complex. Michelangelo originally built them before a siege, and they were later made into an actual fortress in 1553 under Cosimo I.

MUSEUMS

Florence's palaces, churches, and monuments are the creation of some of the most revered artists and architects ever. As the cradle of the Italian Renaissance, Florence is also home to some of the world's most beautiful and important museums, including the museum with the highest number of yearly visitors in all of Italy. Let's discover the six not to be missed.

Galleria degli Uffizi

Universally known as "Gli Uffizi" ("The Offices"), this is Italy's most visited museum, with over two million accesses in 2022, which is more than the Vatican Museums in Rome. The sheer number of historic masterpieces of priceless value on display in its rooms is mind-blowing. To name a few of the most recognizable artists, visitors will find large altarpieces by Cimabue (b. 1240) and Giotto (b. 1267), two of the biggest names in late Middle Ages painting. There are works by Masolino (b. 1383) and Masaccio (b. 1401), two painters who were among the initiators of Renaissance art in Florence. Both *The Birth of Venus* and *Allegory of Spring* by Sandro Botticelli (b. 1445), one of Renaissance's greatest artists, are kept here.

Another world-famous painting is the diptych of the Dukes of Urbino by Piero della Francesca (b. 1412), a giant of art capable of infusing his time's intellectual and philosophical ideas into his creations. Not to mention the only autographed painting by Leonardo da Vinci (b. 1452) – the eclectic genius towering over the entire Renaissance –, a beautiful *Annunciation* from his youthful period. The Flemish school is represented by works by Pieter Paul Rubens (b. 1577), his pupil Antoon van Dyck (b. 1599), and the master of Baroque Rembrandt (b. 1606). The Venetians Giambattista Tiepolo (b. 1696), Canaletto (b. 1697), and Francesco Guardi (b. 1712) are perfect representatives of Italy's eighteenth-century art. And let's not forget the collection of Hellenistic sculptures or artwork by giants of art such as Raphael, Correggio, and Titian. The list goes on.

The building itself, right next to Palazzo Vecchio, was designed by Giorgio Vasari on a commission from Cosimo I when he was Duke of Florence, before becoming the first Grand Duke of Tuscany in 1569. It was conceived as a space where a number of administrative offices could be housed (hence its name), with grand ducal workshops and even some private rooms for the grand duke and his family. Construction started in 1560 and was mostly completed within five years. The Galleria is part of a larger state museum complex called Gallerie degli Uffizi – in Italian, Gallerie is the plural of Galleria – which also comprises the Vasari Corridor, Palazzo Pitti, and the Boboli Gardens, conceived as its grand palace garden.

Palazzo Vecchio

Besides being the seat of city government, a role it has been holding for over seven centuries, the "Old Palace" is also a fascinating museum worth visiting. The Salone dei Cinquecento – the Hall of the Five Hundred – is one of the grandest rooms to be found in Italy. It owes its name to its role as the meeting hall of the Great Council, Florence's main governing body, composed of one thousand five hundred citizens who came together one-third at a time. 177 feet (54 meters) long and 75 feet (23 meters) wide, its walls are covered with large frescos depicting the city's military successes over rivals Pisa and Siena. The stunning ceiling is made of thirty-nine wood panels created and painted by Giorgio Vasari and his workshop. They show important episodes in the life of Cosimo I, first and foremost, a scene of glorification as Grand Duke of Florence and Tuscany, and some views of Florence and its neighborhoods.

This room is also famous for something that cannot be seen anymore: *The Battle of Anghiari* by

Leonardo da Vinci and *The Battle of Cascina* by Michelangelo, two frescos by Renaissance's most prominent artists by far which were either covered or destroyed during the renovations ordered by Cosimo I de' Medici starting in 1555. Thankfully, a different work by Michelangelo still graces the room: *The Genius of Victory*, a beautiful marble sculpture standing in the central niche on the room's southern wall. Additionally, an abundance of artwork in the form of frescos, statues, and tapestry grace this majestic hall.

Several other richly decorated and historically significant rooms are part of the visit to Palazzo Vecchio, such as the Monumental Quarters, the Study of Francis I, and the Halls of Leo X, Clement VII (the two popes of the Medici family), Cosimo the Elder, Lorenzo the Magnificent, and Giovanni dalle Bande Nere, Cosimo I's father and the only military leader of the Medici House.

Palazzo Pitti

Located in Oltrarno, not far from Ponte Vecchio, this stately palace fit for a king is home to no less than six different museums. The wealthy banker Luca Pitti – a rival of the Medici family – started work on this incredible mansion, the largest and most lavish private residence in the city at the time, in 1458. Sadly, the enormous debts incurred to support his dreams of grandeur and the fading of his political fortunes meant he had to stop the construction

86

before the palace was finished, in 1465. Still, the Pitti family took residence in the mansion in 1469.

Cosimo I de' Medici and his wife Eleonora di Toledo – the daughter of the Viceroy of Naples – purchased the palace in 1550 to make it the primary grand-ducal residence. Thus, Palazzo Pitti quickly became one of the more visible symbols of the unassailable power of the Medici dynasty over Florence and Tuscany. Over its long history, this vast mansion was inhabited by two other royal families, the Habsburg-Lorraine – who succeeded the Medici as rulers of the Grand Duchy of Tuscany – from 1737 to 1860, and the Savoy, who took up residence in Florence during the short interlude of the Tuscan center as the capital city of the newly formed Kingdom of Italy, from 1865 to 1871, before King Victor Emmanuel II could finally relocate to the Quirinal Palace in Rome previously inhabited by the pope.

Among the six museums occupying the Palazzo – the Palatine Gallery, the Imperial and Royal Apartments, the Treasury of the Grand Dukes, the Museum of Russian Icons, the Gallery of Modern Art, and the Museum of Fashion and Costume –, the Palatine Gallery is arguably the most impressive one. It includes the most extraordinary collection of late Renaissance and Baroque art, with works by Titian, Tintoretto, Caravaggio, and Rubens, and the most extensive assortment of artwork by Raphael in the world. If you visit, you should not miss the marvelous Boboli Gardens.

Palazzo Strozzi

An astounding fifteen buildings in the city center, including the homes of several prominent citizens, were razed to the ground to make place for this grandiose construction. Like so many beautiful mansions in Florence, it was the realization of a wealthy banker's dream – Filippo Strozzi – who wished to give himself and his family a residence worthy of their amazing wealth. This palace, in the form of a splendid cube with a central courtyard, is widely considered one of the most representative buildings of the Renaissance and a masterpiece of Florentine civil architecture.

The Strozzi family had been exiled from Florence in 1434 for its opposition to the all-powerful Medici but were allowed back in 1466 after amassing a fortune as bankers in Naples, which made them the second richest Florentine family, after the Medici themselves, of course. Ultimately, this majestic city palace was their immortal legacy to their beloved hometown. Nowadays, Palazzo Strozzi is the site of numerous exhibitions and artistic events.

Galleria dell'Accademia

A short walk to the north of Florence's cathedral, the Accademia Gallery is also known as the Museum of Michelangelo. That's because it has more sculptures by the giant of the Italian Renaissance on display than any other museum in the world. Among them, his *David* – one of Florence's symbols in the world and an absolute masterpiece –, the *Four Slaves* (or *Prisoners*) – unfinished statues initially created for Pope Julius II's tomb in St. Peter's Basilica in Rome –, his sculpture of St. Matthew, also unfinished – which was meant to be the first in a complete series of the twelve apostles to be used to decorate the dome of Santa Maria del Fiore –, and the *Palestrina Pietà*, of uncertain attribution. While the Accademia Gallery keeps the original *David*, two copies can be seen in the open: the one in piazza della Signoria and another one placed in the middle of piazzale Michelangelo, an elevated setting offering panoramic views of the city and river.

Other notable works of art on display include the original plaster model of the stunning *Ratto delle Sabine* by Giambologna – the finished statue stands in the Loggia dei Lanzi in piazza della Signoria –, masterpieces by Botticelli – such as the *Madonna and Child* and *Our Lady of the Sea* –, and works by Filippo Lippi, Pietro Perugino, Pontormo, and Agnolo Bronzino, among others. The Museum of Musical Instruments is located in the same building.

Museo dell'Opera del Duomo

This museum, located in the northeastern corner of Piazza del Duomo, is one of a kind. Here, you can take a journey of discovery through the cathedral's stages of development and the artists and architects involved in its rise. At the heart of the museum is the

Sala dell'Antica Facciata (the Hall of the Old Façade), dominated by a colossal model of the cathedral's ancient façade by Arnolfo di Cambio, which was started in 1296 but never completed, ending up being destroyed in 1587.

Works by Donatello, Lorenzo Ghiberti, and Arnolfo di Cambio grace the halls of this fascinating museum, as well as the *Pietà Bandini* by Michelangelo, one of the great artist's latest sculptures.

* * *

There are too many other museums in town to count, and not without reason. As one of the most important cultural hubs in the history of the Italian peninsula and the very heart of that incredible crucible of marvelous art and architecture that was the Renaissance, Florence offers a never-ending collection of artistic masterpieces and sheer beauty, on display both in the open, on the beautiful streets and squares often packed with tourists, and in countless museums, big and small. Depending on your interests and how much time you have at your disposal, the choice is yours.

From the same author

Rome – Its History, Its Art, Its Landmarks

Athens – Its History, Its Art, Its Landmarks

Venice – Its History, Its Art, Its Landmarks

Italy's Finest – Rome, Venice, Florence (Omnibus edition)

Las Vegas The Grand – The Strip, the Casinos, the Mob, the Stars

Made in United States
Troutdale, OR
03/21/2024

18652718R00061